Ir

Comfort for Your Empty Arms and Heavy Heart

Amy Baker
with Daniel Wickert

New
Growth
Press
www.newgrowthpress.com

New Growth Press, Greensboro, NC 27404
www.newgrowthpress.com
Copyright © 2013 by Amy Baker and Daniel Wickert

All Scripture quotations, unless otherwise indicated, are taken from the *Holy Bible,* New International Version®, NIV®. Copyright © 1973, 1978, 1984 by International Bible Society. Used by permission of Zondervan. All rights reserved.

Cover Design: Faceout books, faceout.com
Typesetting: Lisa Parnell, Thompson's Station, TN

ISBN-10: 1-939946-33-6
ISBN-13: 978-1-939946-33-1

Library of Congress Cataloging-in-Publication Data
Baker, Amy, 1959–
   Infertility : comfort for your empty arms and heavy heart / authors Amy Baker with Daniel Wickert. — First edition
       pages cm
   Includes bibliographical references and index.
   ISBN 978-1-939946-33-1 (alk. paper)
   1. Infertility—Popular works. 2. Infertility—Psychological aspects. I. Wickert, Dan, 1955– II. Title.
   RC889.B285 2013
   616.6'92—dc23   2013018363

Printed in Canada

21 20 19 18 17 16 15 14   2 3 4 5 6

Jenny always loved children and grew up as the neighborhood babysitter and big sister. Even as a preschooler Jenny spent hours playing with her dolls. Unlike her friends who might leave their dolls lying around, Jenny was always meticulous in the care of her babies. They were coddled and loved during the day, and at night they were tucked in with tender care. As she got older, Jenny transferred her attention to real babies. She loved working in the nursery at church and was so responsible that she began babysitting before most of her peers. It may have helped that she had three younger siblings whom she mothered and loved too. It was always Jenny's plan to get married and have a house full of kids. She couldn't wait to be a mother—her hope chest was full of baby bottles and blankets.

After high school Jenny went to college and met Mark, the man of her dreams. When they married six weeks after graduation, Jenny was incredibly happy. Although they planned to save some money before beginning their family, they both wanted to have a large family. After two years of saving, Jenny and Mark began trying to have a baby. You might suspect what happened: Jenny was not able to conceive and carry a baby to term.

Despite their lack of children, Jenny's desire didn't die. She still looked longingly at baby clothes and told herself she wouldn't mind if she were sick during the whole nine months of her pregnancy.

When her best friend became pregnant, Jenny cried for a week. Having a child became Jenny's consuming passion. She was willing to try any kind of treatment, regardless of how costly or painful it was.

As time went on and she was still unable to conceive, Jenny withdrew from working at the church's nursery and Wednesday children's clubs. She hid all their books on parenting and frequently refused to go to activities where children would be present. Her husband Mark suffered too. He was also sad that he and Jenny hadn't had children. He wanted to help and comfort Jenny, but nothing he said or did seemed to help. So mixed with his sadness was a feeling of helplessness.

Their problem of infertility is not one Mark is able to solve. They both are praying that God will give them children, but they are starting to lose hope that God hears their prayers and will help them. Their arms are empty, and their hearts are heavy.

Infertility Brings Suffering

Perhaps you can relate to Jenny and Mark. Or maybe your story is much different than theirs. But no matter what the actual circumstances of your infertility, it has brought intense suffering into your life. You may have always assumed that your future would include children, and you structured your hopes around this desire. You thought that, like most of your friends, at the right time you would welcome children into the world. You thought you would cuddle them as babies, watch their first steps, teach them to play ball, send them off to school with a lovingly packed lunch, attend soccer games and piano recitals, help with home-work, and save for college. Now it looks like you may never have that opportunity and you wonder, *Who am I?*

Your friends from school seem to be moving on with their lives, taking the birth of their children for granted. Of course they don't mean to be hurt-ful, but it's painful for you to hear stories about the cute things the kids said or how potty train-ing is going. You know they are just sharing their lives, but still you feel isolated from those you once shared joy with.

Infertility is also painful in other ways. Medical interventions can be costly and time-consuming. Your hopes are raised with each new procedure and dashed with the onset of each new period. You may grieve openly while your spouse may grieve silently. Perhaps you even blame each other for your inability to conceive. It adds up to a strained relationship with your closest friend.

Medically, infertility is defined by a couple unsuccessfully trying to conceive for a year. Statistically about fifteen percent of couples who try for a year will not conceive. Contributing fac-tors could be male, female, or both. It is possible for there to be more than one factor contributing to the problem, and in some situations it is impossible to determine contributing factors. But medical definitions and statistics sound hollow when they apply to you.

Like the author of Psalm 6, you may be crying out, "My soul is in anguish. How long, O LORD, how long?" (6:3). It doesn't matter to you what the percentages are, you simply know you can't have a baby and you long for a child so badly you can taste it. Perhaps like the psalmist, you have cried yourself to sleep on more than one occasion.

> I am worn out from groaning;
> all night long I flood my bed with weeping
>   and drench my couch with tears.
> (Psalm 6:6)

As each month ticks off on Jenny's biological clock, Jenny wrestles with the pain of her suffering and wonders why God would allow her to have such a strong desire for children if he planned to withhold them from her. Jenny has heard plenty of parents complain about their children, and she wonders why God didn't withhold children from them.

Jenny and Mark often ask God

> Why?
> How long?
> Don't you care?

Sometimes they ask angrily, sometimes with despair, sometimes with a deep sadness and mourning. Are these your questions too?

God Speaks to Your Suffering

God isn't silent in the face of your suffering. He wants you to come to him with your questions and your grief. As you do, he answers you through his Word and through the life of his Son, Jesus. When God speaks to us in the Bible, it is the God of all comfort who speaks. He acknowledges openly that the sufferings of Christ flow over into our lives (2 Corinthians 1:5). This honest admission provides ground for trust to grow. God isn't trying to cover up, minimize, or gloss over your suffering. God doesn't bait us with the promise of a pain-free life and then fail to deliver. Instead, the God of all comfort shares in our suffering. When we cry out in agony, we are crying out to a God who is deeply familiar with suffering; he willingly suffered for us at the cross where he carried *our* sorrows, and now he joins us in our suffering and walks with us through deep waters (Isaiah 43:2).

It is in the midst of suffering that we are most prepared to understand the overflowing comfort that comes through Christ. One of the redemptive aspects of suffering is that it can open our ears to hear God speaking words of comfort through the Scriptures. Listen to his words to you.

Do not be dismayed, for I am your God.
I will strengthen you and help you;
I will uphold you with my righteous right
    hand.
(Isaiah 41:10)

This message of comfort was originally offered to Jewish people taken into captivity and deported to a foreign nation. Torn from their families and everything familiar, they suffered intensely. God comforts them with the promise of his love and care, "Do not be dismayed, for I am your God." This comfort is available to you as well. God is still your God. He will strengthen and help you.

You might have already noticed that God's ways and comfort do not always take the form we expect. Rather than giving us exactly what we want at the moment we want it, God offers himself as a superior desire. God offers himself to you as the One who is able to satisfy your deepest longing and deliver your greatest joy. He offers himself as the One who gave his life for you. He is the suffering Savior, the slain Lamb who is worthy to receive glory, honor, and praise (Revelation 5:12). His power can bring light to our darkest moments and deliverance to our bleakest hours.

Consider turning to Jesus and offering him your trust. Your infertility has brought great disappointment and even bitterness into your life, but as you come to know Jesus personally, you will find his words long ago to the Jewish people apply to you as well. "'You will know that I am the LORD; those who hope in me will not be disappointed'" (Isaiah 49:23).

The Lamb to whom you offer your trust is the lover of your soul, the One who makes a way through the barren desert of your life, and provides streams to refresh you as you travel through this desert. He allowed himself to be led to slaughter so that your wounds could be healed.

In his letter to people undergoing intense suffering, the apostle Peter begins with praise for Jesus, the Lamb of God. Does that surprise you? Most of us wouldn't expect a letter to sufferers to begin with praise. Yet that's how Peter began. Look where Peter finds hope. "Praise be to the God and Father of our Lord Jesus Christ! In his great mercy he has given us new birth into a living hope through the resurrection of Jesus Christ from the dead" (1 Peter 1:3).

Peter continues, "[In this birth] you greatly rejoice, though now for a little while you may have had to suffer grief in all kinds of trials" (1 Peter 1:6). It is *this birth* which can provide your deepest satisfaction and joy, comfort you in your darkest moments, prevent bitterness and anger from consuming you, and strengthen you to persevere and even become a light to others stumbling in darkness. This birth allows you to transfer your gaze from your disappointing and painful circumstances to your Savior. Looking upon the One who was crushed in exchange for your life causes your new birth to become your living hope and greatest joy.

As a result, rather than being trapped in suffering, you can begin to take a different look at your infertility. As you long for a change in your family, you can also long for a change in your heart. God's promise of hope and comfort isn't dependent on a change in your circumstances. Listen to what Peter says produces inexpressible and glorious joy.

> In this you greatly rejoice, though now for a little while you may have had to suffer grief in all kinds of trials. These have come so that your faith—of greater worth than gold, which perishes even though refined by fire—may be proved genuine and may result in praise, glory and honor when Jesus Christ is revealed.
> (1 Peter 1:6–7)

Peter explains that inexpressible and glorious joy results from a faith in Christ that longs to see Jesus receive praise, glory, and honor.

While the suffering of infertility wrenches cries of pain from the childless, infertility simultaneously offers opportunities for something else to occur. The suffering of infertility offers a taste of Christ's suffering and creates an opportunity to be devoted to him, his glory, and his kingdom. The greatest gift of all is not having a child, but being a child, *his* child. And continued suffering offers a continued reason to long for Christ to come and to set our hearts on things above, where the barren will have joy eternally. In his presence we find eternal pleasures.

Peter goes on to encourage the sufferer. "Prepare your minds for action; be self-controlled; set your hope fully on the grace to be given you when Jesus Christ is revealed" (1 Peter 1:13). Let's explore some ways you can "prepare your minds for action" in the middle of your struggle with infertility.

Prepare Your Mind for Action

All the suffering we experience brings the same temptations that Adam and Eve experienced in the garden of Eden. "Is God good?" "Can he be trusted?" "Is he withholding from me something I need for life?" And of course there is the temptation to blame God and others for our circumstances. Questioning God's goodness and love or blaming God and others when things go wrong are responses natural for everyone. But turning to God in faith when we suffer great disappointment and tragedy is supernatural. That can only happen when we have experienced the new birth that Peter is talking about.

But our new birth in Christ doesn't take the pain and struggle of our disappointment and suffering away. That's why Peter calls us to prepare for action. Now we can struggle in a different way. We struggle to turn away from our natural response to suffering and toward the living God who offers us hope, comfort, and the power to love others in the midst of pain and sorrow. But remember we don't struggle alone; our God, through the gift of his Spirit, promises to be with us, to help us, and to strengthen us. Go to your faithful Savior and ask him to help you turn away from your natural response to suffering and toward him. Ask him for the gift of faith.

Turning from Blame

It's easy to be vulnerable to anger and bitterness when you learn that a factor in your spouse has contributed to your experience of infertility. It becomes tempting to see childlessness as the fault of the spouse who has a compromised reproductive system. It can seem like your spouse is the barrier standing between you and your dream of children. Sometimes arguments can follow in which careless, painful words are tossed around like grenades. "It's your fault . . ." "If you weren't . . ." (And even if you don't say those actual words, you might think them.) Those words and thoughts leave wounds that open the door to bitterness and hurt in your relationship with your spouse. As a result, the two people God designed to become one, splinter and fragment. Rather than reflecting a picture of Christ and his bride, a marriage in which blame is not addressed leads to deep wounds, desolation, and even divorce.

So when Peter warns sufferers to prepare their minds for action, it is a well-placed warning. Heeding the warning can begin as each spouse refuses to see the experience of infertility as *his* problem or *her* problem, but as *their* problem. They are *one*. No longer is any problem they encounter solely the problem of the other spouse. Just as the whole body goes into action when one part of the body is harmed (for example, when a car door is slammed on a hand the whole body reacts), so two people who have become one are to share in each other's suffering. If one falls down the other is there to help.

This can become your opportunity and your privilege in the days to come. When the weight of suffering threatens to suck the life from your spouse, you can softly remind your hurting lover of the faith that is of greater worth than gold. You can gently remind your beloved of the new birth and living hope you have in Christ. You can quietly live out your hope in front of your spouse, knowing that next week it may be that you will need your spouse to do the same for you when the mantle of suffering seems too heavy to bear.

As you prepare your mind for action, you will want to remind yourself often of the mighty power of God. He who was pierced for our transgressions and crushed for our iniquities is powerful enough to heal all wounds. He offers the amazing promise that he will work everything in our lives for good;

he will use every circumstance to conform us to the image of Christ. In allowing you to experience infertility God has entrusted you with the opportunity to become more like this perfect Savior who is the essence of all that is beautiful and good.

Turning toward Your Spouse

You can also prepare your mind for action by meditating on the truth that God wants your spouse to be your primary earthly relationship. This will be the case even if God blesses you with children, so guard your relationship now. Invest as much effort in building intimacy and friendship with your spouse as you invest in trying to build a family.

You'll especially want to guard your sexual relationship. When you are trying to conceive, it's easy for your intimacy to become regimented. Sex is scheduled during the most fertile part of your cycle in order to create the most favorable conditions for getting pregnant. There is nothing wrong with that, but God's intention for sex to be pleasurable and fun and an opportunity to bring your spouse great pleasure, may get lost in the regimen of sex to get pregnant. Sex may become an obligation and become associated with continual disappointment.

God wants sex in marriage to be pure and holy (Hebrews 13:4). Following God's guidelines for sex, therefore, might be considered an act of worship. Do you view your sexual relationship with your spouse as an act of worship, or over time has your view of sex become solely associated with conceiving? In 1 Corinthians 7 God teaches that the primary goal of the sexual relationship is meeting the needs and desires of the spouse. Love seeks to give for another's benefit. Guard your union by training yourself to cherish your spouse and think of your marriage as your most treasured earthly relationship.

Turn from Centering Your Life on Conceiving

Those suffering with infertility can be tempted to become obsessed with getting pregnant. As this obsession slowly takes control of your mind, you can start to build your whole life around getting pregnant and having a baby. When obsession takes over, you may become unreasonably angry if your husband is called out of town on business during the most fertile part of your cycle. You may go deeply into debt for procedures and medical treatments that hold the hope of allowing you to have a child. Your only joy in life may be the possibility of being pregnant, and your deepest sorrow may be childlessness.

When this happens, God feels distant and harsh. In the Bible we read that Job also felt like this. Job told God, "Why do you hide your face and consider me your enemy?" (Job 13:24). Job wrestled with why he was suffering, concluding in his human wisdom that he would be better off if God left him alone. "Withdraw your hand far from me, and stop frightening me with your terrors" (Job 13:21). Perhaps you have been tempted to conclude the same thing.

However, after having a direct conversation with God, Job decided that there were things "too wonderful for me to know" going on in his situation (42:3). Are you willing to trust that there are things too wonderful for you to know going on in your situation as well? If so, rather than desiring God to go away and leave you alone, you can draw near to him with the full assurance that he will draw near to you in goodness, gentleness, and compassion. James 5:11 says, "You have heard of Job's perseverance and have seen what the Lord finally brought about. The Lord is full of compassion and mercy."

You can begin to comprehend the beatitude in Matthew 5:4, "Blessed are those who mourn, for they will be comforted." God tends his flock like a good shepherd and carries the lambs close to his heart (Isaiah 40:11). Allow him to gather you in his arms, and be close to his heart.

Be Self-Controlled

Peter also encourages sufferers to be self-controlled. What might that mean in the context of your struggle with infertility? Below are some thoughts. Perhaps you can think of others as well.

Show Self-Control by Continuing to Love and Minister to Others

With the pain of unfulfilled dreams for a family, it can be easy to withdraw from others. Being around children seems to keep the wounds open, a constant reminder that others have what you want. And if the mere presence of children didn't make life hard enough, well-meaning (or not so well-meaning) relatives and friends add to your distress with their inevitable questions about when you are going to start a family. Sometimes it's subtle: "Joe and Tina's daughter just gave them their first grandchild." Sometimes it's blatant: "You've been married for five years now, what are you waiting for?"

But avoiding family gatherings doesn't provide safety from prying questions. It can feel like every time you meet someone new their third question is, "Do you have children?" (Right behind "What's your name?" and "Are you married?") You feel like family and strangers alike all want to know what's going on in your bedroom. It's tempting to withdraw; your wounds are painful enough without making yourself vulnerable to others.

However, because of your new birth into the living hope of Jesus, by God's grace you can be a person known for loving and serving others. The Old Testament illustrates this by telling us about an infertile woman known only as "the Shunammite" (2 Kings 4). This woman and her husband had likely lived with infertility for many years (the woman's husband was described as old). Yet this woman's identity does not seem to be wrapped up in her infertility. We come to know her in the passage as a woman who shows hospitality to Elisha and asks her husband to build an addition to their house so that Elisha could stay there whenever he came to town.

Most of us have never had anyone build an addition on their house just for us to have a nice place to stay when we visit. Elisha was understandably grateful and looked for some way to show his gratitude. Unsure what the perfect gift would be, Elisha told his servant to find out what the Shunammite would like to have. But when the servant asked, the woman replied that she wanted nothing; she was completely content.

Nevertheless, Elisha was still determined to do something for her. At that point, his servant observed that the Shunammite was childless. Elisha didn't waste any time in calling the woman to him and promising her that she would have a son. The woman's response indicates that Elisha had touched an area where she was vulnerable. She pled with Elisha not to build up her hopes if she would later be disappointed (2 Kings 4:16).

Notice four things about this woman from this passage:

- She was childless.
- Infertility was an area in which she was vulnerable.

- She ministered to others and sought to make life better for them, rather than making life better for herself.
- She was content.

Apparently she had not allowed her infertility to cause her to withdraw from people or from ministry. Following the example of this woman will require self-control on your part, but be encouraged by the fact that self-control is part of the fruit of the Spirit you have living within you. Because the Spirit is living in you, you have continual help. You can ask the Spirit for daily, hourly, minute-by-minute grace to live out the self-control, which is the Spirit's gift.

Showing this self-control will probably require advance planning on your part. What will you say to Aunt Biddy when she asks why you aren't starting a family? How will you reply to the person to whom you've just been introduced who asks if you have children?

Allow love and graciousness to guide you in framing your responses. If you are mindful of the Lord's great mercy in giving you a new birth, such questions may become your opportunity to demonstrate your faith in the midst of suffering, and as a result bring honor to Jesus Christ. God may also use your faith in suffering to draw others to himself so that while you may not nurture biological children, you can have the privilege of nurturing spiritual children. This is the call of the new covenant—to go and make disciples by sharing the good news of salvation through Jesus with your words and your deeds. As you focus on ministering to others, you will find that your sense of contentment grows as well.

Over time, you may find that you're able to minister to children also. Perhaps you and your spouse have already discussed some of these options. These are personal decisions, and every family will come up with different ideas. The main thing is to think through how, given both of your gifts, strengths, and abilities, you can be a blessing to others. Whatever you decide, be assured that as you move forward in faith, God will grow you to be like him and use you to be a part of growing his kingdom.

Show Self-Control by Setting Boundaries

For those wanting to begin a family, a number of treatment options are available and constantly evolving. Researching your options may require a significant investment of time. And some treatments will cost thousands of dollars. It will be easy to continually pursue the next suggested treatment with hope that you will be able to achieve your goal of starting a family.

It will require self-control not to be consumed with your desires. It will take self-control not to go deeply into debt to pay for various treatments. And it will take self-control not to blindly agree to treatments that you could not agree to on ethical grounds—if your desire for a child was not so strong.

It will be important for you and your spouse to establish boundaries. Determine together how far you will go. Determine how much you will do in order to get pregnant, and establish some cutoff points. This will be different for every couple so it's important that you and your spouse discuss and set boundaries together. While it may be helpful to learn what other couples have done, you and your spouse will likely have factors to consider that vary from those of other couples. It may be wise to get help from a biblical counselor as you set your boundaries because it's often difficult to think objectively about things that are deeply personal and close to your heart.

Set Your Hope on Christ

Finally Peter encourages all believers undergoing any kind of suffering to set their hope fully on the grace they will receive when Jesus is revealed. Jesus is your Savior, the Son of God sent by God the Father to do what good parents do for their children—sacrifice themselves. Because of his sacrifice, your greatest hope must not be in having children; it must be in knowing and loving your Savior. Just as your parents knew that walking was better than crawling, your heavenly Father knows that faith is better than human desires. Faith in

Jesus results in a *living* hope, a hope that will certainly come to pass.

You understand what it's like to want to love a child who hasn't been born. You understand what it's like to anticipate the joy caused by the birth of children. Use your understanding to deepen your love and joy in Christ. Notice what Peter says next.

> Though you have not seen him, you love him; and even though you do not see him now, you believe in him and are filled with an inexpressible and glorious joy, for you are receiving the goal of your faith, the salvation of your souls. (1 Peter 1:8–9)

Set your hope *fully* on the grace to be given you when Jesus Christ is revealed. Move toward your Savior; don't turn from him in your suffering. While your perseverance may or may not end in being a joyful parent, your suffering is not in vain. As you draw near to Christ, your suffering will certainly result in praise, glory, and honor when Jesus is revealed.

CROSS YOUR
LEGS AND WISH

CHRISTOPHER PILLING

REDBECK PRESS 1994

Other books by the author

Snakes & Girls (New Poets Award, University of Leeds School of
English Press 1970)

In All the Spaces On All the Lines (Phoenix Pamphlet Poets Press 1971)

Foreign Bodies (Flambard Press, Newcastle upon Tyne 1992)

Acknowledgements

I gratefully acknowledge George MacBeth's airing of a flock of these
birds with birdsong on BBC Radio 3 in 1971 and 72 and Peter
Porter's finding a niche for 18 of them in the P.E.N. Anthology:
New Poems (Hutchinson 1972). Thanks too to the editors of Ambit,
Child Education, Four Poetry & Audience Poets, the Halifax Courier,
Headland, the Lancaster Festival Anthology 1990, New Hope
International, the New Statesman, Pennine Platform, Phoenix,
Phoenix Pamphlet Poets and the Times Literary Supplement where
others, or fledglings of others, have appeared.

Thanks to John Barnard, *Wren & Owl* flew off as a new poets award
broadsheet.

The first line of *The Wordpecker* . . . was a poem written in our
visitors' book by Bryony Pilling when just turned five. All those
who stayed the night had a poem to write.

The drawing on the front cover and the lettering of *Gannet* on page
27 are by Shelagh Collins.

for Sylvia

Sylvia & Sol arise
And all is day

Ich bin der dreiarmige Leuchter
Vom wissenden Vögeln bewohnt
Mit dem siebenfarbenen Blick

Ivan Goll: *Hiob*

La terre s'arrête un moment de tourner,
prise entre les genoux des grands fleuves,
emmêlée dans les vols d'oiseaux
qu'elle organise de village à village.

Lucien Becker: *Plein Amour*

If you see a flock of birds you must cross your legs and wish.

A superstition in Rutland
Opie: *The Lore & Language of Schoolchildren*

CONTENTS

The topiarist

I   *Topiarius* has the bird he wants
unless the clippers slip,

unless he can't quite tell
without standing back

the length of
the curve of

the neck, the slant of the bill.
And it can perch on a green balaclava.

II There are only so many
birds he can have,

so many shapes he can turn
to his account,

so many sizes
he can appropriate,

so few colours
of hedge plumage

but innumerable nuances
in the mind's eye view.

The naturalist

I recognise this wren because it looks like other
wrens. The common traits should be taken for granted
and idiosyncracy praised. I am sure I know my brother
better. His mind is much like mine or naturally demented.

The swift: *'Der Weibsbild, dat zarte Bild,*
              Wiel's in de Karke geit!'

The martin: *'Wenn du siehst, wenn ik seh,*
              Wenn se Middags in ehr Köken steht,
              Süt seut as de Düwel in de Hölle.'

Woman combing
and posting hairs
through the high window slit
for the martins' employment.

Woman rinsed & turbanned
may not be the pretty picture
the swifts claim to see
as they swoop past the lychgate.

Woman swooping downstairs
remembering the roast,
and how do the martins know
of her *csárdás*

with castanets & the carving fork?

The dipper

comes to a gill and carries on walking along
the ground onto the bed of the stream,
the slaughter of insects its dream.
From a rock over rapids its mate clinks a song.

Lapwings

Flesh-brown legs: pattering on the field.
The field is covered in snow.
Rumps: dark green shot
with purple. Crests: which do not yield
to the astringent wind.
They lord it, they strut, they're on show.

My lady, got
up in high black boots, white-starred tights
and navy duffel coat: thinned
by the icy air. The lights
and warmth of the Library Van
staved off the chill a while.

Now for an awkward moment she's pinned
with *Exotic Birds* and *The Ascent of Man*
to a rickety stile.

Snowflakes start to fall: undisciplined.

Garden warbler

One *Sylvia* is well hidden
in the foliage. Unbidden,
she clucks and goes on clucking:
chek chek chek chek chek . . . from the undergrowth.
Upstairs with the other ducking
under the bedclothes
– a breath of fresh air for us both.

Stonechat

Get near, it will let you!
Watch the gorse doesn't attack
– its spines are out to get you!

The stonechat's squeaks and alarm
– *weest trak trak* –
will keep you well away from harm

you hope as you try to press
closer to the attractive black
head, white rump and chestnut breast . . .

Let the yellow gorse upset you!

Mistle thrush

disturbed, cuffs the bramble camouflage
– Is it immune to thorns? –
clattering into the air
to let its feather sense the danger pacing near
– tell-tale snap of twigs,
persiflage of leaves –

Can you hear
truEEtrüwu . . . *chuREEchuRU* . . . *chüWÜtru* . . . *churuwüTRÜ*
and a final twittering?

Blackbird

Yellow beak tweezers balls of honeysuckle.
Seeds swallowed, crop full, it sings
– the flowers' scent is memory –
a bouquet for its territory.
The fullness of time is red and sticky.

Carrion crows

I   There are two crows on a playing field of snow.
     Winter games are cancelled. It is significant

     That they have come as a pair, having been drawn
     Together, stay jabbing in unresisting whiteness.

     Two black birds scoring the candour of the mind.

II   The mending tailor shot at a crow.
     Caw! Caw! the carrion crow!
     Such derring-do hey derry dido
     For a sedentary tailor to wield a bow.
     He shot wide of the mark; he pierced his sow
     Right bang through the heart. He respects crow now.

III   The bird watcher is vigilant lest one stray
     Be hung from barbed wire for all to mime
     Lest the world's black crows turn into clay

     A random crow moves finely out of time

Fieldfares

Near rowans the dead stay under the earth.
Fieldfares pluck *cock-drunks* from these trees;
replete, the comb on wood of their voices
is as if the buried had cause for mirth.

Red-backed shrike

Butcher bird, Jack baker, Wariangle
impales nine insects before it ends its fast.
The stuck muses are powerless to untangle
their black arts from the brake of thorns.

Then the shrike *breaks bread;*
                              they sing, stabbed.

Green woodpecker

Before its sharp beak picked holes in an oak trunk
you set a fire in to smoke the devil out
you ended up coughing and reeling like a drunk,
burning your thumb. The woodpecker fell about.

Cuckoo

I   Jesus asked for a loaf – he'd scented new bread.
The baker rejoined: 'I'll sell you one instead.'

But his wife and six daughters offered him the batch,
secretly, of course – you wouldn't catch

them letting their husband and father know
how generous they'd been. But Jesus knew, and so

he made them into stars: the Seven Sisters. Heaven
rejoiced. The baker was made a cuckoo. No leaven

could have restored his livelihood after their deed.
He depends on others now, according to his need.

II   His mate visits certain warblers by day. 'Match
the shade and markings of your egg to theirs,' he said,

choking, but don't lay as many as seven!'
Of course, his words only came out in *cuckoo*.

By starlight hear the whispers from reed to reed.

Linnet

Small birds may take a cuckoo for a sparrowhawk
and mob it.
Small boys may find a linnet's nest
and rob it.
Let's hope the egg they take – the big one – will not talk
and tell them:
'I'm a cuckoo or about to be.' It's best
if they blow
the albumen and yolk away
and not know
at all that it's their cuckoo day.
But a little bird may tell them.

Goldcrest

's

persistent siss in a Lawson's cypress

Blue tit

The blue tit flew higher than it normally does
because of my presence
near the feeder. I went indoors. Once
there the boy I was watches it fly straight to the low fence
which cuts my land from the neighbour's.
If she's watching too its colour and jinks
are simultaneous
for us both, that is, unless she blinks.
How that tit got to where it is may be common sense,
but does she know I've been in the garden past tense?

Tree-creeper

A tree-creeper nested in his tumble-down shed
behind a heater.
He – a carpenter – let it breed
undisturbed.
Then he drank half a litre
of whiskey, thinking he'd been given the bird.

Kestrel

still
on the *qui vive*

```
T       s
h   b   i           u
e   l   l   h   n
    a   i   i   i
b   c   c   s   s
r   k   l   s   o
o       e       n
o       s   i
m           n
s
```

                                    for the kill.

Jay

Who'll teach
the jay to screech?
I, said the Virginia creeper.

We require a deeper
jar, said the scrawny owl,
throwing in the towel.

Up there in the ring
the box tree took a wild-goose swing
and mist

came down over the jay blue *Alpes des Maures*.
The jay blew a foghorn offshore
by default

as it screeched to a halt.
Oakum
all ye faithful acorns, my eardrum

needs no caulker.
I'll teach you to squawk a
round, said the jay walker.

The common tern

has nothing on its mind. It has a direction
and understands the sea, which has no moods
but changes. It takes advantage of the wind;
does not feed in the sea's whipped albumen.

Black-headed gulls

Just to have counted the black-headed gulls
behind the birches on the playing field
would have been something to do. Counting lulls
with definite answers. And finite ones.
I was looking beyond the birches, eyes peeled
for something far less precise (*here the ink runs
and smudges*). As the gulls took off they wheeled . . .

Skylark

Song of skylark in each subtle
Tumble of wind – risen essence
Of moorland.

        The crested bird descends
And the heath is brown expanse:
Burnt umber bracken, numbed fibrils.

Out of waste, skylark ascends
In dry eddies of warbling.

Chaffinch

> This chaffinch is worth a cow.
> Harz proverb

Je suis le fils d'un riche prieur.
Qui est-ce qui veut venir à Saint Symphorien?
In pllein, pllein, pllein, p'tit plât de roûtie.
Fi, fi! les laboureux, J'virrons ben sans eux!
Oui, oui, oui, oui, je suis un bon citoyen.

Yellowhammer

Yellow buntings are not nefarious.

Yet Scottish youngsters, taught
that their eggs were *'gouted with the taint
of the de'il's blood',* sought
them out, to sever the head
of every unfledged naked *yite*
clean off with a thread.
It would turn the stomach of a saint.
'We're *spanging* the *gorbals,*' they said.

They held each tight
and in a blood-curdling parody
of a *gold spink*
in flight – *'steuf, steeLIT, twink* . . .
            'Get out of our sight,
            the parents ranted,
            an' the de'il tak ye!'
. . . and *the de'il de'il de'il de'il tak ye,'*
the children chanted
as they raced to the barn and hilarious
deeds fit only for night,
flapping their arms in a vicarious
send-up of a headless and featherless *skite.*

Or so I'm told.

How could this brilliant bird's hold
on life be so precarious?

Wren & Owl

Wren fetched fire from the pleasance of heaven
for man, sun napalming its skin.

                              Owl
had no feather to offer. Its eyes raven
and sear. Dive-bomber, it lives in a hole.

Magpies

I   There are no magpies in the forest of Gavre.
      Brittany waved them away, sky's flat fish
      expelled for revealing Anne to the English
      by pecking her hide-out, hide of a dead horse.
      Thus the legend.

II   And, undulating, God said: 'Have
          for discovering her, seven of the devil's hairs.'

III   Out of its high fork, a pied bird is easy prey
      for a holey carcase of duchesses
      who are raving. Becoming one with carrion is
      a given way to make a magpie ravenous.

Nightingale

The eyes and heart of a nightingale laid about men in bed
keep them awake. Eat the heart and sleep

will only ever last two hours – you'll be like the bird
in the blackthorn thicket. Hear the parade of the sleep-

less ganglia, the bagpiping, the jug jug jugging, the loud
pioo, the strutting tune demanding a reward.

The wind shifts. Instead of the thorn-pricked bird or sleep –
across the heath, maddening, hear the red fox pad . . .

Mute swan

She is not turning to a swan, this Leda,
now she will entertain the god
who comes by dream to tread her.

Swan floats whitely; or turning, welds
with woman's arm. Or is wrought gold.

Woodpigeon

I've only to take my eyes off
her farthingale
for a fleeting second
– the time for a hoop-snake to flick
into the undergrowth –

and one of those sing-song pigeons
takes it into its beak
to peck at my eardrum
– is it after the blood of the
burrowing hoop-bee?

There, see, she's swivelled and gone
and I'm left in the throes . . .
– not even a chance
(*too-zoo, cushat, cushiedoo*)
of hoop-la on her lawn.

House sparrows

One on another's backbone, flapping elaborately.
O such a shadow! Such butterfly contractions of sunlight!

Thrush

on a tightrope for its exuberant evening song.
(It's the telephone wire I talk to you along.)

Raven

entente
    conjugale
benedict
    benedicite
song of the
    three children
is a sunbeam
    unbroken by
a thrown cup
    but blessed
by a tumbling

    raven

Eagle or Dove

The brazen Fiery Serpent stings you into Life,
hissed God to Adam. Clippings (nail, wing) waylay His
lust. Keep your talons in, fluff your gold feathers, Wife.
Draw His sacred flame-forks with your damper kisses.

Hoopoe

Swabian hoopoes bring the magic springwort
to open bunged cavities. That's its virtue
for hoopoes in search of a nesting site. *Squirt
the juice from springwort if you'd like something new
and exciting.* It's already covered in dew
but no less explosive. If you take off your skirt,
that red one, why don't you? and throw it on the ground
the bird will think it's fire. If you knew
that fire is its element, you'd want to do
just that, wouldn't you? The hoopoe will be bound
to drop its find – far more efficacious than rue –
and think what *you* could do with magic springwort!

Fulmars

I think I'll put to sea.
The children are
777777777777777uuuuuuuuuuuuuuuuuuuuuuuuuuuuuuuuuuuuuu
uuuuuuuuuuuuuuuuuuuuuuuuuuuuuuuuuuuuuuuuuuuuuuuuuuuuuu
uuuuuuuuuuuuuuuuuuuuuuuuuuuuuuuuuuuuuuuuuuuuuuuuuuuuuu
uuuuuuuuuuuuuuuuuuuuuuuuuuuuuuuuuuuuuuuuuuuuuuuuuuuuuu
uuuuuuuuuuuuuuuuuuuuuuuuuuuuuuuuuuuuuuuuuuuuuuuuuuuuuu
uuuuuuuuuuuuuuuuuuuuuuuuuuuuuuuuuuuuuuuuuuuuuuuuuuuuuu
uuuuuuuuuuuuuuuuuuuuuuuuuuuuuuuuuuuuuuuuuuuuuuuuuuuuuu
uuuuuuuuuuuuuuuuuuuuuuuuuuuuuuuuuuuuuuuuuuuuuuuuuuuuuu
uuuuuuuuuuuuuuuuuuuuuuuuuuuuuuuuuuuuuuuuuuuuuuuuuuuuuu
uuuuuuuuuuuuuuuuuuuuuuuuuuuuuuuuuuuuuuuuuuuuuuuuuuuuuu
uuuuuuuuuuuuuuuuuuuuuuuuuuuuuuuuuuuuuuuuuuuuuuuuuuuuuu
uuuuuuuuuuuuuuuuuuuuuuuuuuuuuuuuuuuuuuuuuuuuuuuuuuuuuu
uuuuuuuuuuuuuuuuuuuuuuuuuuuuuuuuuuuuuuuuuuuuuuuuuuuuuu
uuuuuuuuuuuuuuuuuuuuuuuuuuuuuuuuuuuuuuuuuuuuuuuuuuuuuu
uuuuuuuuuuuuuuuuuuuuuuuuuuuuuuuuuuuuuuuuuuuuuuuuuuuuuu
uuuuuuuuuuuuuuuuuuuuuuuuuuuuuuuuuuuuuuuuuuuuuuuuuuuuuu
uuuuuuuuuuuuuuuuuuuuuuuuuuuuuuuuuuuuuuuuuuuuuuuuuuuuuu
uuuuuuuuuuuuuuuuuuuuuuuuuuuuuuuuuuuuuuuuuuuuuuuuuuuuup

wards and a handful.
Errant souls, never at rest.
And far louder than you think.

I'll glide long distances on stiff straight wings
imagining I'm going places.

I only have something to say at home
when the stink's died down.

Mal Mock, Molly Mawk, John Down, it's after 7 o'clock:
– Up to bed, you lot!

Shag

Corrodent sea is white and gnawing, sea-grey
and oiled enough to lock the shag in feathers,
heaving in efforts to be lurched to land
for restlessness to cease and ease to be.

Oyster catcher

pie de mer

k
e
e
b
e
k
k

p i n k - l e g g e d

m u s s e l - p e c k e r

s k i l f u l   o y s t e r - s p l i t t e r

shallow bowed wing-

beat

slow

low

over water

Jackdaws

But in these nice sharp quillets of the law,
Good faith, I am no wiser than a daw.
Earl of Warwick in the Temple garden
(Henry VI Pt I)

Christmas and the jackdaws are quarrelling
on our lawn. 'That fat is mine!' 'That fat is mine!'
With each beak gunbarrelling,

each beady eye – even though there are twice as many –
fails to see us carolling
and the greedy seagulls lift the bacon rind.

When their war is over, there isn't any –
not any war, not any fat, not any sign
of what they had in mind.

Flamingo & Marabou

Grow, flamingo, do, or the marabou will get you:
hollow pouch at its neck, ugly adjutant is deadly
still, stock still. Flex your sticks before the fix;
fly, flamingo, plane, or marrowbane will bayonet.

Quail

weet my feet
wet my lip
quick me dick
paye tes dettes
j'ai du blé; j'ai pas de sac
tres pour un; tres per un
ta-tatataye

The quail lack a sense of smell
to tell the human from the quail,
to know the male from the cloak
trailed by hunters out for the kill.

The quail-caller is a human
(human?) artifice for men
to cull the quail from Spain
before they leave the brown

protection of their nest
of grass to catch the air east
from Tarifa to Moroccan waste.
They are split open on toast.

Pied wagtail

I   Rue
the day, *Wattie-loo!*
The cuckoo who

made
no nest, laid
an egg, invaded

the
half-hidden summer
squat of you inno-

cent
two who only want
a brood of confident

twitch-
tails, not an eldritch
intruder which

would
snitch much good
Willie Wagtail food . . .

II Rue
the day, *Washer-woo!*
Young cuckoo who

left
the nest bereft
of your young, having deftly

edged
your fledglings
out into the sedge,

true
to its calling, outgrew
your home and dispensed with you.

Cuckoo!

Sedge warbler

The rank bog does not deter
the sedge warbler on the osier.

Robin

My father killed a robin.

His sow was like to be piggin';
she bore a litter of seven,

that died.

Three brothers have a fever
– and father is a-dyin'.

Heron

Jack Hern will not send a Valentine.
Expert at poised intention, stalking
for the jab, his swift feminecine
movements take the place of sweet talking.

Bee-eaters

The brilliance of their colours
can at a distance be dull as
anything unless the sun comes out of hiding.

You would not know how *peau de soie*
their undulating patterns are
unless you spy them swooping and gliding.

Lory

Butterflies alight with spread wings, bask:
peacock on buddleia, wallbrown and gate-
keeper on paths we walk. Or when you glance
away close to.

                I do not have to ask
questions of them. But they do not expatiate
like Salvadori's lory.

Royal wood nymph humming bird

hovers: with a straw
for a tongue, sucks
down nectar
and minute fizzing insects
from an overlapping
crimson fuchsia
ear drop.
It needs sustaining
each quarter hour.

Toucan

The tou
can
has a cap
acious can
oe
beak, light with honey
combs
of air. The fru
it it
cap
sizes are heady
with plummet
ing domes.

Nightjar

The burring dor hawk
Wordsworth

Who would have thought the nightjar
an imbibing bird, a sucker of goats?
Who would have thought your thought
was of the digestion of the wind-eater?

Goat-sucker, *engoulevent*, the soul of a child
unbaptised! Gabble-ratchet! What incredible beliefs!
Or a spinning wheel heard to churr at dusk
on lazy summer evenings in Nidderdale.

House martins

intensely wheeling before the set-in facade
of the College of Education
– you'd think they were trying to enter.

They keen,
            flash in droves,
                            casually ovoidal.
            And their centre?
The open?

The students lazily gaze at their lecturer's
known closed features.

Starlings

The jovial gardener with his sickle
edge-down against his shoulder
plods to other meadows.

                         Taking off, fickle
starlings crescent in wide glinting
metallic blades
             or make even bolder . . .

One's come tumbling down
our chimney. It's thrown
us, caught us unawares.
It's thudding against the
bow window it cannot see.

And now it's off up
to the attic, on the hop.
Who's it think it is? Where's
it think it's going? Quick, catch
it and throw it out, dispatch

the poison in the neck of stares.

Swallows & Sparrows

Swallows stole the nails; apprehensive sparrows
flew them back, then cried '*jif! jif!* (He is alive!)'
if the soldiers slept. Atonement for sparrows goes
like this: hop hop hop hop hop hop. Swallows dive.

Goldfinch

The goldfinch as a mere reminder of Christ's death
won't do. Red-faced, it tinkles from the thistle fluff.
It does not eat thorns. Its song takes all its breath.
It pecks out the seeds before they fly. That is enough.

A wordpecker . . .

A wordpecker flied out of a hole.

                                      'Prick
up your ears, it said, unless you've reckoned
that because I drum fast for a good half-second
at a time and often, it's sound that makes me tick.
That or spruce seeds. I'll fly them to a stump
or cavity in a tree trunk and thump
them till they open ccccccccccccccccccccccccccc
                        ccccccccccccccccccccc
                        ccccccccccccccc
                        ccccccccc
                        ccc
                        c
                        l
                        i
                        c
                        k
                        .
                        ;

Notes

The epigraph from Ivan Goll's *Job* runs: I am the three-branched candelabrum inhabited by knowing birds with the seven-coloured look.

Carrion crow: Section II relies on this folk song:

THE CARRION CROW

A carrion crow sat on an oak;
　Hey derry down, derry dido:
Watching a tailor mending his cloak;
　Caw! caw! the carrion crow:
　Hey derry down, derry dido.
O wife, O wife, bring here my bow;
　Hey derry down, derry dido:
That I may shoot this carrion crow;
　Caw! Caw! the carrion crow:
　Hey derry down, derry dido.
The tailor he fired, but missed his mark;
　Hey derry down, derry dido:
For he shot his old sow right bang through the heart;
　Caw! Caw! the carrion crow:
　Hey derry down, derry dido.
O wife, O wife, bring brandy in a spoon;
　Hey derry down, derry dido:
For our old sow is down in a swoon;
　Caw! Caw! the carrion crow:
　Hey derry down, derry dido.
The old sow died, and the bell did toll;
　Hey derry down, derry dido;
And the little pigs prayed for the old sow's soul;
　Caw! Caw! the carrion crow:
　Hey derry down, derry dido.

Chaffinch: the Harz proverb comes from Thuringia where chaffinches were highly prized and highly priced if they were first class songsters. One workman at Ruhla so admired the musical prowess of a particular chaffinch that he gave a cow in exchange for it. Perhaps it was singing the Double Trill, the Wine Song, which went: *Fritz, Fritz, Fritz, willst du mit mir zum Weine gehen?* The chaffinch call has been similarly transcribed in different parts of France, and the five lines come from (i) near Orleans, (ii) in Normandy, (iii) in the Saintonge (*roûtie* is a piece of bread soaked in wine), (iv) in Lorraine and (v) near Paris. Linking them is not solely a sign of inebriation.

Cuckoo: country people in Germany called the cuckoo *Beckerknecht* (the baker's boy), one legend telling how a baker was changed into a cuckoo for refusing to give Jesus a loaf and the baker's wife and daughters who gave it, were transformed into the Seven Sisters, a constellation that would shine so long as the cuckoo sang, i.e. from St Tiburtius's day, April 14th, to St John's, June 24th.

Eagle or Dove: And the Lord said unto Moses: Make thee a fiery serpent, and set it upon a pole; and it shall come to pass, that every one that is bitten, when he looketh upon it, shall live. And Moses made a serpent of brass and put it upon a pole; and it came to pass that if a serpent had bitten any man, when he beheld the serpent of brass, he lived. (Numbers 21 viii-ix) Be ye wise as serpents and harmless as doves. (Matthew 10 xvi).

Fieldfares: *cock-drunks* and *hen-drunks* were local names for rowan berries in Cumberland. Probably drunk on tarn water.

Fulmars: once called Mollemawk in Yorkshire, Malmock in the Shetlands (from the Dutch for foolish gull), John Down in Newfoundland and Fulmar (Foul marten) because of their noxious vomit over intruders at the nest. Along with many sea birds that never seem to rest, they used to be known as âmes damnées (damned souls) by French sailors.

Goldfinch: sometimes featured in paintings of the Madonna and Child because of the erroneous belief that they feed on thorns as well as thistle seeds.

Green woodpecker: their territorial call in Spring is full-throated laughter, hence it was known as Laughing bird or Yaffingale. When God had finished creating the earth, He ordered the birds to excavate hollows destined to become seas, rivers and pools. All obeyed except the obstinate woodpecker. Her lot was to be ever pecking wood, but my woodpecker has the last laugh.

Heron: known as Jack hern in Sussex. Saint Valentine's Day falls during the breeding season.

Hoopoe: like the woodpecker, often considered to be a lightning-bringer. In Swabia (now a part of S.W. Germany) the hoopoe brought the mysterious springwort, whose root caused doors and rocks to fly open. To procure it, plug the hole of a hoopoe's nest and kindle a fire or put a red cloth on the ground beneath and the bird, having flown off for the magic herb, will think it has to return the plant to the element from which it sprang: i.e. lightning-fire, and will drop it after use in order for it to be burnt up.

Jackdaws: in Bohemia it was believed, may be still is, that if jackdaws quarrel among themselves there will be war.

Jay: characterised by sudden raucous shouts, striking plumage and a fondness for acorns, which it swallows whole, as I hope you will the poem! In Brittany it was thought that jays building in oak trees cannot be tamed, because they are liable to the falling sickness!

41

Magpies: after the battle of St Aubin du Cormier, Anne, Duchess of Brittany, the last sovereign of that country, was betrayed to her enemies the English by the magpies, who, when she was concealed in the carcase of a horse, pecked holes in the hide and disclosed her place of concealment. As a punishment God expelled them for ever from the forest of Gavre. Bretons did not look kindly on the magpie and declared that seven of the devil's hairs grew on its head.

Mute swan: Leda, pregnant, was seen bathing by Jupiter. Struck by her beauty he resolved to deceive her. He persuaded Venus to change into an eagle, while he became a swan. He fled from the cruelty of the bird of prey into the arms of Leda, who sheltered him. He made love to her and in time she produced two eggs; from one sprang Pollux and Helena, from the other, her husband's offspring, Castor and Clytemnestra.

Nightingale: medicinal folk lore from Brittany has it that if a person eats the heart of a nightingale, he will sleep only for two hours, because that bird sleeps only for two hours in the night. But this is dangerous, for if the wind changes in the twenty-four hours, he runs the risk of going mad. Sir Thomas Browne considers in his "Vulgar Errors" 'whether the nightingal's sitting with her breast against a thorn be any more than that she placeth some prickles on the outside of her nest, or roosteth in thorny and prickly places, where serpents may least approach her'.

Nightjar: a popular belief that it sucked the teats of cows and goats and caused them to go blind was prevalent in France and Germany as well as in Britain (*Tette chèvre, Geismelker, Goat sucker*). Another French name for the bird, *engoulevent* (wind-gulper) is probably because when caught it opens an enormous mouth and spits like a cat. Its whirring sounds led to names like Eve churr and Scissor grinder. The country people in Nidderdale called them gabble-ratchets (corpse-hounds) thinking nightjars embody the souls of unbaptised infants doomed to wander for ever in the air. Gabble-ratchets, more properly applied to clamorous geese circling at night, is a corruption of Gabriel or *gabbara* (corpses) *racches* (dogs which hunt by scent and give tongue).

Oyster catcher: its provincial names include mussel pecker, and sea pie or, in French: *pie de mer*. A shrill keBEEK keBEEK as it flies, means, according to Campbell (West Highland Tales) 'be wise' though he spells it: Bi Glic, Bi Glic (*Bee-Gleechk*) and has oyster catchers say it when a stranger comes near their haunts.

Pied wagtail: called *Wattie wagtail* because it frequents ponds and streams, *Washerwoman* because its tail bats the washing, and *Willie wagtail* in the Orkneys.

Quail: *weet my feet* etc. are all names for the quail (Scottish, Irish, English, French and Swiss) derived from its call-note.

Raven: Saint Benedict, sent a poisoned loaf by a priest envious of his sanctity, commanded a tame raven to carry it away beyond the reach of any living creature. Benedict is a name for a newly married man, especially one who has long held out against matrimony. *Benedicite,* bless you, as well as a grace at table, is the opening of the canticle: *Benedicite omnia opera* from The Song of the Three Holy Children. To see one raven was accounted lucky, three the reverse.

Red-backed shrike: known as Butcher bird generally, Jack baker in the S.E. and Wariangle (Worrying or Destroying angel) in Yorkshire. The German name *Neuntödter* tallies with the reason for it being called the Butcher bird in Britain: 'it always kills and impales nine creatures before it begins its meal'. Despite being impaled, the muses don't die.

Robin: based on the words of a miner from the West Riding of Yorkshire.

Starling: the diminutive of 'stare'. In the Hebrides it was supposed by hunters that there was poison in the blood of a starling's neck.

Swallows and **sparrows:** based on a Russian legend. For their sins, sparrows have had their legs fastened together by invisible bonds.

Swift and **martin:** originally this duologue in Old High German was about a farmer's wife from the Harz. The church swallow (swift) says: 'Look at that picture of a woman, that pretty picture, how she walks into church.' And the house swallow (martin) responds with: 'If you saw her as I see her, in her kitchen at midday, you'd think she were the very devil in hell.'

Woodpigeon (or **Ring dove**): farthingale comes from the Spanish for 'hooped'. *Too-zoo, cushat, cushiedoo* are names derived from its coo.

Wren and **Owl:** a version of a Breton legend (recounted in *L'Artiste*) runs: It was necessary for a messenger to fetch fire from heaven to earth; and the wren, weak and delicate though he was, cheerfully undertook to perform the perilous mission. The brave little bird nearly lost his life in the undertaking, for during his flight, the fire scorched away all his plumage, and penetrated to the down. Struck with such unselfish devotion, the other birds, with one accord, each presented the wren with one of their feathers, to cover his bare and shivering skin. The owl alone, in philosophic disdain, stood aloof, and refused to honour, even with such a trifling gift, an act of herosim of which he had not been the performer. But this cruel insensibility excited against him the anger of the other birds to such a pitch that they refused from that time to admit him into their society. And so he is compelled to keep aloof from them during the day, and only when night comes on does he dare to leave his melancholy hiding-place.

Yellowhammer: this bird, the gold spink, called the Devil's bird, the yellow yite or skite in Scotland, was reputed to drink a drop, some said three drops, of the devil's blood each May morning. The Scottish equivalent of *little-bit-of-bread-and-no-cheese* was *de'il, de'il, de'il tak ye.* According to Swainson: 'Scotch children hang by the neck all the yellow ammers they can get hold of. They often take the bare *'gorbals'*, or unfledged young, and suspend them by a thread tied round the neck to one end of a crossbeam, which has a small stone hung from the other. They then suddenly strike down the stone and drive the poor bird into the air. This operation they call *spangie-hewit.*'

Details of most of the bird lore are from 'The Folk Lore and Provincial Names of British Birds' by the Rev. Charles Swainson, originally published by the Folk-Lore Society in 1885 (Kraus Reprint 1967).

This edition is limited to 350 copies of which 26 have been lettered
A – Z and signed by the author.

Cross Your Legs and Wish
0 946980 20 9

This book is published by Redbeck Press, 24 Aireville Road, Frizinghall,
Bradford BD9 4HH. Design and print by Tony Ward, Arc/Littlewood
Press, Nanholme Mill, Shaw Wood Road, Todmorden, Lancashire
OL14 6DA.